Covenant Bible Study Series

Love and Justice: A Biblical Understanding

Eva O'Diam

Brethren Press
Elgin, Illinois

Covenant Bible Study Series
Love and Justice: A Biblical Understanding

Copyright ©1990 by Brethren Press

Brethren Press, 1451 Dundee Avenue, Elgin, IL 60120

Cover design by Jeane Healy

Library of Congress Cataloging in Publication Data

O'Diam, Eva.
    Love, compassion, and justice: a Biblical under-
standing/Eva O'Diam; foreword by June Adams Gibble.
        p. ca.—(Covenant Bible Study series)
    ISBN 0-87178-542-9
    1. Justice—Biblical teaching—Study and teaching. 2. Caring—
Biblical teaching—Study and teaching. 3. Love—Biblical teaching—Study and teaching. 4. Bible—Study. I. Title. II. Series.
BS680.J8035 1990
241—dc20   90-42964 CIP

Manufactured in the United States of America

Contents

Foreword

"The Lord told us what is good. What the Lord requires of us is this: to do what is just, to show constant love, and to live in humble fellowship with our God" (Mic. 6:8). The prophet Amos reminds us, "Let justice flow like a stream, and righteousness like a river that never goes dry" (5:24). In response to these familiar passages of scripture, we ask, "How?" How are we to *do* justice? How are we to show *constant* love?

As persons of faith, how do we understand "justice" in our day? And what is our relationship to the justice system in our country? First, we recognize that there are many differing understandings about justice and love in today's world. And then we admit that, even in our diversity, we can come together to explore the scriptures and learn more fully what God is calling us to do.

The Christian community has a unique message to share. This message is grounded in the biblical understanding of justice as a restorative process rather than one that is primarily punitive or rehabilitative. Restorative justice begins with the understanding that God created and pronounced creation "Good!" Within creation God provides wholeness — a sense of completeness. True justice seeks to restore that wholeness to all persons and all situations. The heart and soul of justice is discovered in community, and the restoration of relationships happens within community.

This study of love and justice is designed to help us look in new ways at the biblical concept of justice and love, the system of justice in our country, and our personal responses to God's call to do justice.

Welcome to this relational Bible study which is designed for small group settings within the congregation. As your group begins this study, you will want to keep in mind some important features of relational Bible study.

1. The words of scripture relate to our lives and become alive for us today;
2. Each person contributes to the study . . . each one shares the meaning that they find and helps bring meaning to others;

3. All persons are learners and all are leaders . . . we all come needing to learn; we help lead each other to new discoveries;
4. Trust and vulnerability are needed . . . we are vulnerable as we share out of life's experience; in relational Bible study, we learn to trust others and to be trustworthy;
5. Together a small group of learners gathers around the Word and discerns God's word for them today.

Relational Bible study has a strong biblical foundation. It is anchored in the covenantal history of God's people. We believe that God's empowerment comes to the community as its members gather to pray and to study, to share, to receive, to reflect, and to act. The gathered community is necessary for growing up in faith. Yet such growth does not just happen—it must be struggled for in the power of the Holy Spirit and in accord with the teachings of Jesus Christ.

Relational Bible study takes seriously the corporateness of our faith. The body of Christ becomes a reality within the life of the group. Each person's contribution is important as the group seeks the meaning of the text. "For just as the body is one and has many members, and all the members of the body, though many, are one body, so it is with Christ . . . . Now you are the body of Christ and individually members of it" (1 Cor. 12:12, 17).

Relational Bible study helps both persons and the group to claim the promise of the Spirit, to be open to the active working of the Holy Spirit in their midst. "For where two or three have met together in my name, I am there among them" (Matt. 18:20). "For God did not give us a spirit of timidity but a spirit of power and love and self-control" (2 Tim. 1:7).

May you know God's presence and power as you study the biblical message of love and justice and consider its meaning for today. May God's grace and peace guide you in your listening and your speaking, in your differences and your agreements, in your struggle and your growth. And may we all continue to grow into deeper understandings of how God calls us to live out love and justice in today's world.   June Adams Gibble
Elgin, Illinois

About the author:

Eva O'Diam has been a probation officer and Church of the Brethren pastor. She is recruitment coordinator of Prisoner Visitation and Support for federal and military prisons (an alternative interfaith ministry).

1

A Prophetic Vision
of a Just World
Isaiah 32:15-20

Preparation

1. Individually reflect and write on some or all of the following questions. What needs to happen for this new world to come into existence? How would you define freedom? What needs to happen in your life for you to be free? What does it mean for us to be God's children? If peace ruled, justice prevailed, and righteousness flourished, what would our world be like? What would we be like? Take time in your group to share one another's dreams.

2. Read Isaiah 32:15-20 in several translations: the Revised Standard, the New International, the New English, and the Jerusalem Bible. List other words that are used for peace, righteousness, and justice.

Understanding

A friend calls with an urgency in their voice, "I am in a real fix. Can you loan me some money?" The reasons for needing money could be many. Perhaps your friend took out a loan thinking that some money would arrive before a payment was due, but it didn't. There may have been a medical emergency in the family. Maybe the bills have simply piled up and need to be paid. Name any reason. Imagine any amount of money. It could be $5 or $1,000 or $5,000—as long as it is an amount that makes you stop and think. How would you respond? Probably, most of us would help if we felt the need was real and our friend promised to pay back the debt.

What happens though when the debt is not paid back? You can approach your friend and demand payment. You might drop hints, hoping they will catch on and remember to pay you. Another possibility is that you might forgive the debt and tell them they owe nothing. Which solution offers justice?

When I was a probation officer, I dealt with the case of a 16-year-old charged with an accident that resulted in the deaths of a family of four: a mother, father, and two children. The teenager had fulfilled the requirements and received a driver's license only weeks before. After school one day, the teenager decided to see what speeds the car could reach. The teenager drove down a back country road at a high rate of speed and met the family of four in a fiber glass recreational vehicle. Being an inexperienced driver, the teenager could not control his car and hit the family, killing all of them.

When the case came to court, the teenager pleaded guilty. As probation officer, I was asked to make a recommendation to the court for sentencing. Both the family who was killed, as well as the teenager, came from faithful church families, respected in the community. A strong outcry for justice came from both sides. Friends of the family who had been killed felt that the only justice for the teenager was to serve time in jail. Friends of the teenager felt that nothing could be accomplished by a jail sentence and that the only justice for the teenager was to live with what had happened and to perform services in the community. The law permitted either plan. How could justice be rendered?

Your definition of justice determines your answer. Few of us spend hours reflecting on the subject. In fact, we find it difficult to define justice. Often reflections on justice require us to consider the injustices present in our society. We think of the homeless, those in prison, the refugees, AIDS victims shunned by family and friends, and acts of violence caused by racism, sexism, homophobia, etc. None of us likes to be reminded of such events. Examining justice requires us to look at our own prophetic witness (or lack of it), how we view relationships with those people, and the prejudices we carry. Is it any wonder God's prophets who cried out for justice felt so alone?

Yet those prophets, like Isaiah, knew the source of true justice. Isaiah knew the prophetic vision for a just world could grow from the transforming power of the Spirit of God: "Until the Spirit is poured upon us from on high, and the wilderness becomes a fruitful field, and the fruitful field is deemed a forest. Then justice will dwell in the wilderness, and righteousness abide in the fruitful field" (Isa. 32:15-16). Only with the outpouring of the Spirit of God can justice be born and only in justice is there the hope of the new age dawning.

If the source of justice is God, then, the substance of justice is righteousness. Justice and righteousness go hand in hand. Even Webster defines justice as "the quality of being righteous." Indeed, Isaiah recognizes that as justice dwells, righteousness will abide.

For years I struggled with the concept of righteousness, until someone shared with me a way to visualize it. It may be helpful to visualize it in the same way. Picture a cross. The vertical bar of the cross reminds us of our relationship with God. The horizontal bar reminds us of our relationship with each other. Righteousness calls us to fulfill the demands of our relationships both vertically with God and horizontally with one another. Both are necessary for righteous living. Neither alone will be sufficient.

Isaiah, however, does not stop there. "And the effect of righteousness will be peace (*shalom*), and the result of righteousness, quietness, and trust for ever. My people will abide in a peaceful habitation, in secure dwellings, and in quiet resting places" (Isa. 32:17-18). Peace or *shalom*, as many of us know, may be translated as completeness or wholeness. The circle stands incomplete without mention of the *shalom* which results from the fulfilling of our relationships. Thus, the circle is complete as we understand that peace of any kind is a wholeness, a completeness given by God.

There can never be a prophetic vision for a just world apart from an understanding of community life. Justice pours out from God upon all who meet the demands of relationships. God demands our complete love with all our heart, soul, and mind and that we love our neighbor as we love ourselves. Apart from this there is no justice, no righteousness, no peace. With this love God creates fairness, impartiality, fulfilled relationships, completeness, and wholeness.

Was Isaiah writing only of a world to come or a present possibility? When we look around at our world and see the injustices that surround us, we tend to comfort ourselves by removing Isaiah's vision to a future reality. Even if we really believed that it is a present possibility, we tend to throw up our hands in despair and say that one person cannot possibly make a difference.

But how much difference *can* one person make? A folk song reminds us, "One man's hands can't tear a prison down. Two men's hands can't tear a prison down. But if two and two and fifty make a million, we'll see that day come 'round. We'll see that day come 'round." Even as the prophet knew that justice, righteousness, and peace must always be addressed within the context of community, we too must address those issues together.

In this study, we will look at the biblical concept of justice. We begin with Isaiah's vision of a peaceable world—a world in which everyone and everything fit rightly and are treated justly—a world we are to help fashion—together.

Discussion and Action

1. In the beginning of this session, you were invited to name other words that are used for justice, righteousness, and peace. How do you define these words?

2. In the situation with the teenage driver, how could justice best be accomplished? What feelings do you think the teenager carried? How would you respond to family members? How would you respond to the friends of the teenager?

3. Injustices occur in all our lives. When I reflect on growing up, I can remember a number of small injustices. Some people have had major injustices occur. Do you remember a time when you felt an injustice in your life? Who was involved? What primary issues were at stake in your life? Was justice achieved?

4. Earlier you envisioned a new world—a just world. Could your vision become a reality? Why or why not? Is there some small step you could take to make that vision a reality?

2

Zealously Pursue Justice
Deuteronomy 16:18-20

Preparation

1. Look at a magazine or newspaper to find pictures of people of various races, occupations, and backgrounds (e.g., a Black businessperson, a Caucasian preacher, a street person, an Hispanic father or mother with children). Place the pictures in front of you and write your assumptions/descriptions about each person. Would you feel comfortable speaking to them on the street? If they were walking behind you, how would you react? Where do you imagine they live? What are their goals and their dreams? What do you believe their greatest needs to be?
2. Read Deuteronomy 16:18-20. The personification of justice is usually a blindfolded goddess holding the scales of justice and a sword. What do these symbols represent to you?

Understanding

"You shall appoint judges and officers in all your towns which the Lord your God gives you, according to your tribes; and they shall judge the people with righteous judgment" (Deut. 16:18). Little is known of the Israelite legal system. According to *Eerdmans Handbook of the Bible*, "There was no great division between civil and religious law in Israel. Priests, Levites and elders worked to the same end and shared the administration of justice. The gate of the city or village was the place where grievances were aired and cases formally judged." Judicial systems were commanded by God and indeed viewed as a gift from God given to God's people for true justice to reign.

Judges served in order to "judge the people with righteous judgment. You shall not pervert justice; you shall not show partiality; and you shall not take a bribe, for a bribe blinds the eyes of the wise and subverts the cause of the righteous" (Deut. 16:18-19). The sole aim of justice was to restore community, to enable wholeness to be restored when relationship demands went unfulfilled. Judges were not to be persuaded by a person's personal background, and they were never to receive money from either party whom they were called to judge. Concern was for the one who had been wronged in the relationship, and restoration of the relationship was a priority.

In New Testament times, the Sanhedrin served as the supreme court. Roman authorities allowed them to pass any sentence under Jewish law with the exception of the death penalty. Still, local disagreements were settled at the gate by city elders, and the intent of the judges remained steadfast—to restore the community, to bring forth righteousness, to fulfill the demands of relationships.

The concern of justice was the victim. In a relationship, the victim was the one who fulfilled responsibilities within the relationship while the other party did not. Victims complained against their offenders and brought them before the judicial system. Sanctions were not so much a matter of punishment as an attempt to restore the relationship.

This system fell by the wayside, however, when kings began selling writs. Victims buying writs purchased the king's services in bringing the offender to justice. If a citizen bought a writ, the king's court would file the charges, argue the case, and see that the offender was brought to justice. Thus began the system of justice we now practice where there is little concern for the victim, for restoration of relationships, or for rehabilitation. Instead, our criminal justice system has become a state monopoly where the crime rate rises, the powerful are served, and the poor and powerless are punished.

Recently, Dr. Nicholas Kittrie, speaking to a conference on services to Jewish prisoners, shared some startling facts:

> Every year 40 million serious offenses are committed. Of those 40 million offenses, 12 million are reported. Of those reported, 2.25 million are arrested, 1 million stand trial, and 700,000 are convicted. Of the 700,000 that are convicted, 2% or 14,000 actually serve time in prison.

Do you ever wonder who those 14,000 people are? Visit a courtroom one day. Watch who is convicted. Do those with suits and well-paid attorneys get convicted as often as those with public defenders? Tour a local jail or prison and ask who their average prisoner is. What is the educational level? What is the income level? Dr. Kittrie also suggested that prisons are a sign of a rich society. Only wealthy societies can afford to hire the state to prosecute all criminal offenses. Only wealthy societies can afford to separate offenders from the rest of society and in some cases keep them in remote areas. But can we afford to ignore the fact that 95% of our prisoners will return to society? Can we afford to ignore the racial, ethnic, and sexual discrimination prevalent within the system and damaging to those people?

The Criminal Justice Reform Statement prepared for the Church of the Brethren 1975 Annual Conference states clearly in Section I, "The failures of our present criminal justice system are widely apparent. The rising crime rate is one evidence that the system neither deters nor rehabilitates." It goes on to spell out many areas of concern. Our criminal justice system tends to serve the powerful segments of our society. Thus we will see many more Cuban detainees in our prisons than corrupt government employees. The system tends to protect property at the expense of persons. We often choose to imprison people rather than arranging restitution for crimes against property.

Arbitrary use of power within the system tends to punish the poor and the powerless and free the rich and powerful. When I served as project director for a bail-bond group in DuPage County, Illinois (at that time one of the twelve richest counties in the United States), it was no coincidence that the individuals we served were transient people unable to make bail. Each was represented by a public defender, who would glance momentarily at their file only minutes before the hearing that could change their entire lives. In contested divorce cases or custody hearings, often the person who "wins" is the one who spends the most money on an astute attorney. But where power and wealth often determine the outcome, when people's lives are at stake, can anyone win?

The Criminal Justice Reform paper further reminds us that we, as the public, hold many misconceptions:

Prisons protect us from crime. We continue to build prisons yet the crime rate rises.

Reformatories reform, correctional centers correct, penitentiaries teach penitence, incarceration rehabilitates. At their best, prisons serve as warehouses and punish. At their worst, they are brutal, unsanitary dens.

Most people in prison are dangerous, one must be an expert in criminology to help, and all persons in jail are guilty. People in prison are persons like you and me. They, too, are created by God. They feel alone and are often separated from families. They may or may not have done something wrong and are living the consequences. When things happen in our own lives, we, too, live with the consequences.

Poor people and minority groups are more inclined to commit crimes than others. They are less likely to afford a proper defense and so are more likely to be incarcerated.

We could continue but certainly the picture is clear. God's intention was a fair, impartial system of justice. Indeed, God commanded the Israelites to implement such a system. But that system has strayed from God's intention. How might we respond? We can educate ourselves and others concerning our misconceptions. We can return to an emphasis on the victim and to righteous justice that concerns itself with the restoring of relationships. We can make the return to society rational for those in prison.

Discussion and Action

1. When have you encountered our criminal justice system? Were you a defendant, a witness, a plaintiff, a parent, a friend? Did you ever serve on a jury? Was the system fair? In what ways? What did the encounter have to do with your faith?
2. Are there ways we can work at making the victim the central focus again? What does it mean today to have righteous justice as the aim of our criminal justice system?
3. During this study, you may want to remember people in your congregation and community who have been victims, prisoners, or employees in the criminal justice system.

3

Law and Covenant
Exodus 19:1-6

Preparation

1. Read Exodus 19:1-8. Reflect on the meaning of covenant in your life. What does it mean for you to be in a covenant relationship with someone? List each relationship in your life that you would define as a covenant relationship. Describe the positive as well as difficult aspects of those relationships. Is it possible to walk away from a covenant relationship? If so, how might that happen? If not, what does it mean to remain in a covenant relationship with someone whom you dislike?

2. For the Israelites, the Exodus and Sinai experiences were symbols of the covenant relationship between Israel and Yahweh. And in their worship experiences the Israelites repeated that history over and over again. Remember and share a time when you were most aware of your covenant with God.

Understanding

I grew up in a Christian environment and I remember times when I was less than a perfect child. Once I threw a baseball at the wall in our house and made a good-sized hole (the walls were very old). Another time I stayed out until 2 a.m., when my mother expected me home much earlier (of course, I had a great explanation). And then there were the many times when I pulled my younger sister's hair, fought with her over what television show we would watch, or became angry with her and called her names. My mother used to tell me as she disciplined me, "I'm doing this for your own good. This hurts me more than it hurts you." Such instruction and discipline could come from my parents because of the covenant we shared. No, I guess I wasn't the perfect child, and at times I needed some instruction and some discipline. We all do. If we are to grow in self-understanding, in knowledge, and in our faith, we continue to need instruction and discipline through our lifetime. Such instruction and discipline can be most effective when it happens within covenant, when we are instructed and nurtured by each other.

Our growth depends on studying the scriptures for application in our daily living, on our willingness to share who we are, and on our openness to understanding others.

The Hebrew word for covenant, *b'rith*, carries the meaning of bond or agreement. Historically, the origin and development (etymology) of this word is unclear. Covenant, as it is used to refer to the bond or agreement that God established with the Israelite people, was borrowed from social usage (*The Interpreter's Bible*, "Exodus," p. 841).

In Israeli social practice, two general types of covenants could be established. Some covenants were established between two equal parties. In this type of covenant, two equal parties entered into an agreement where the obligations and the privileges agreed upon were shared equally. Other covenants were established between partners who were not equal. For example, such covenants were established between rulers and their subjects. In these covenants, what was agreed upon was in reality a gift or promise made by the stronger party and conditioned by obligations from the weaker party. Regardless of what was promised, such an agreement did not infringe on the power or the freedom of the one offering the agreement.

Which type of covenant did God establish with the Israelites? Obviously, there was a stronger and a weaker party. God offered the covenant as a gift. The Israelite people acknowledged the power of Yahweh. After crossing the Red Sea, they sang of God's power, and they experienced that power as they traveled through the desert receiving water and manna from God. On Mount Sinai, God told Moses to remind the people of what God had done for them. "You have seen what I did to the Egyptians, and how I bore you on eagles' wings and brought you to myself" (Exod. 19:4). Clearly, God is in charge.

Apparently, God continues to set conditions and obligations for the Israelites to meet. "Now therefore, if you will obey my voice and keep my covenant, you shall be my own possession among all peoples; for the earth is mine, and you shall be to me a kingdom of priests and a holy nation. These are the words which you shall speak to the children of Israel" (Exod. 19:5, 6). This makes the covenant a conditional one. If the Israelites will obey, then they will be God's own. Clearly the initiative for the covenant comes from God. It would seem, therefore, that the covenant was of the second type.

We need to note two important features of the covenant. Even in a covenant where there is a stronger and a weaker party, the weaker party has the ability either to accept or reject the agreement. Indeed, God only offered the covenant as a gift. God never assumed the covenant as an established fact. If you read on in Exodus 19, this is clearly pointed out. "So Moses came and called the elders of the people, and set before them all these words which the Lord had commanded him. And all the people answered together and said, 'All that the Lord has spoken we will do.' And Moses reported the words of the people to the Lord" (Exod. 19:7-8).

The second point is that it is unclear what was required in the covenant. In the biblical account, the people agree to the covenant before any laws are recorded. Scholars cannot agree on which laws, if any, were part of the original covenant. It is clear that all the laws stress the theocentric, dynamic, and personal nature of their relationship with God. Having established covenant, the purpose of the laws was to state clearly the mutual obligations and responsibilities within the agreement. They were given to teach and to instruct the Israelites the meaning of being God's people and to provide discipline to the learning process.

The Israelites seemed to fight this process quite similarly to the way children often fight this process with their parents. Eventually, with the foreign influence of Canaanite religion, some Israelites came to see the covenant as the first type of social covenant discussed—one between equal parties. They wanted to see themselves as equals with Yahweh—with equal obligations and privileges (again, similar to many teenagers in their feelings toward their parents). They felt God was as dependent on Israel as Israel was upon God. However, this view would tend to limit God's freedom, and the prophets spoke out strongly against these assumptions.

Today, the laws which we follow exist to clarify the mutual responsibilities we have as we live in communities. Most of these are governmental laws, and one could question whether they have any relationship to the covenant we share with God. We understand that with the death and resurrection of Jesus Christ, the law has been fulfilled. Perhaps there are no rules as there were for the Israelites, but in our covenant with God there is the living example of Jesus. That example was given to us that we might be instructed and, yes, even disciplined in our faith.

Discussion and Action

1. Consider the two types of covenants established in Israeli social practice. Do we have both types of covenants today? Can you name some of each? Look at your list of covenants. Can you find both types on your list?
2. What are the advantages and disadvantages of each type of covenant? Which do you feel more comfortable with?
3. What functions do laws have in our lives today? Do you find them helpful? Are there laws that you rebel against?
4. If we were to establish a covenant relationship with God similar to the one of the Israelites, what laws would be important to include? What helps or hinders you in strengthening your covenant relationship with God?
5. What does it mean that Jesus Christ is the fulfillment of the law?
6. In your present covenant relationship with God, what serves to instruct and to discipline you?

4

Forgiveness and Justice
Matthew 18:23-35

Preparation

1. Read Matthew 18:21-35. List the persons who owe you a debt of any kind. What kinds of debts are owed you? How do you decide which ones are important to collect? How do you go about collecting the debts? What happens if someone refuses to repay a debt?
2. List the persons to whom you owe a debt. What kinds of debts do you owe? Are you likely to pay off a debt willingly or wait until someone requests or even demands payment? Are you more likely to repay tangible debts for which there are bills than intangible debts which might stem from what someone has offered you through a relationship?
3. Are there some people you are more likely to forgive than others? Who are they?

Understanding

In the book *Crime and Reconciliation,* Mark Umbreit tells the story of a man named Fred Palmer. Randy and Tanya Brown, newly married, returned from their honeymoon to discover that their house had been broken into and their wedding gifts stolen. Another couple, Randy and Elizabeth Yohn, returning from visiting friends, discovered their house, too, had been burglarized. Both couples felt violated. Eventually police caught the thief, Fred Palmer. He stood trial and received a sentence of ten to twenty years.

During this time a new penal code was being put in place. Although the crime occurred under the old penal code, the judge applied the spirit of the new law, suspending all of the lengthy sentence contingent on Palmer spending 250 days in a maximum security prison, paying restitution to his victims, enrolling in psychotherapy, and remaining on probation for five years. Palmer lived up to all of his responsibilities even meeting face-to-face with each of his victims and paying full restitution.

The prosecutor, however, never accepted the judge's ruling and filed an appeal, contesting the judge's sentence to the Indiana Supreme Court. There it was determined that Fred Palmer was incorrectly sentenced and he was sent to prison to serve his ten-to-twenty year sentence. After having spent close to a year in prison and having been reconciled to his victims, Fred Palmer left his wife and two children and his job to return to prison.

One might ask, where is there justice in this story? Is justice to be found in the fact that the police caught Fred Palmer? Or is justice better found in the judge who felt it best to attempt to rehabilitate a man than to punish his wrongdoing? Or was Fred Palmer the one who practiced justice as he met with his victims face-to-face and made full restitution for his crimes? Or did justice finally prevail when the prosecutor won the appeal, the full letter of the law was carried out, and Fred Palmer was returned to prison?

Remember, as we learned in chapter one, justice and righteousness go hand in hand. Justice reigns when the demands of relationships are fulfilled, whether that relationship is with God or another person. The question that arises, however, is what happens when the demands cannot be met and the relationship cannot be fulfilled? Jesus addresses this question in the parable of the Unforgiving Servant. Do we simply fulfill the letter of the law and live with the brokenness? Or do other avenues exist that deal with the problem?

The parable begins in the midst of Jesus' conversation with the disciples about life in the faith community. It continues the discussion on life within the kingdom of heaven. That "kingdom" carries both a present as well as a future reality. We err at times thinking that because the term *heaven* is used, the kingdom stands as a distant reality. And Jesus' teachings about the kingdom seem to be about the future—not what is expected of us now. Although the full reality lies in the future, Jesus invites the present community of faith to be the kingdom as well. Jesus emphasizes the importance of a simple, humble faith built on trust, concern for those on the fringe of the community, reconciliation between persons who are broken, and a sincere attitude of forgiveness.

Forgiveness is difficult for many of us. According to the *Interpreter's Commentary*, rabbis taught that three pardons sufficed. Peter more than doubled that figure when he suggested seven! However, Jesus said even that was not enough but that one should forgive seventy times seven. For those of us who can multiply, that means we should forgive 490 times. Jesus says that forgiveness has little to do with our calculations. Rather, it is a matter of the heart.

In the parable, the unforgiving servant owed a legitimate debt of millions of dollars to the king. Obviously, the king loaned the servant the money with the expectation that it would be repaid. The servant, who might have intended to begin repaying the debt many times, had ignored the demands of the relationship. The law allowed the king to sell the servant, his family, and all his possessions for the repayment of the debt. The servant requested time. Justice led the king to offer forgiveness, the debt was cancelled, and the relationship between the king and servant was restored.

Abuse of any gift can result in the loss of that gift. The servant, keenly aware of debts after this experience, left the king's presence, looked for a fellow-servant who owed him twenty dollars, and demanded payment. The servant fell to his knees, begging for more time, but the unforgiving servant refused, promptly throwing him in jail, unwilling to offer the same gift he had only moments before received. Law allowed for his response, but the heart and the spirit of justice did not.

When Jesus taught the disciples to pray, he included the line, "Forgive us our debts as we forgive our debtors." The king, hearing about the actions of the unforgiving servant, ordered him back and imprisoned him until he could return the debt. Jesus again teaches, "So also my heavenly Father will do to every one of you, if you do not forgive your brother [and sister] from your heart" (Matt. 18:35).

Are we a forgiving people? Indeed, with Christ's death and resurrection, we are forgiven people. But we cannot *live* as forgiven people, we cannot *be* forgiving people, unless we stand ready to forgive others. How willing are we to forgive?

We tend to forget that some of the greatest people of faith fell short of what God intended. By the state's standards, they could have been in prison. As I began reading through the Bible, I was amazed at the dishonesty of Abraham. Moses murdered an Egyptian (Exod. 2:11). King David ordered the death of Uriah (2 Sam. 11). Saul, later known as the Apostle Paul, persecuted early Christians.

Recently, I participated in a discussion on working with people in prison. One chaplain said that as he worked with prisoners he always recognized that there, except by God's grace, go I. Another person spoke up and disagreed, saying we can never be effective until we realize—*there go I.* We are forgiven people only as we are able to forgive.

Discussion and Action

1. What does "forgive and forget" mean? Is it possible to forgive without forgetting? Can we forget without forgiving?
2. What the law allows may not always be what is just. The law allowed the king to throw the servant in prison. Instead, the king forgave the debt. Can you think of other situations where this might be true? Have you personally experienced this?
3. Jesus taught us to pray, "Forgive us our debts as we forgive our debtors." What meaning does this have for you as you pray it? Why can we only be forgiven as we are able to forgive?
4. How do you view prisoners? Do they deserve forgiveness? How do you see yourself as similar to them? As different from them?
5. Does everyone who breaks the law deserve to be punished? How do you account for Abraham, Moses, David, and Paul? If not everyone deserves punishment, how do you decide who does and who doesn't?

5

Reaching Out with Compassion
Matthew 25:31-46

Preparation

Read Matthew 25:31-46. What do you believe about the last judgment? How does what you believe compare with this parable? Are there similarities? Are there surprises? What is most surprising about Jesus' account of the last judgment?

Understanding

For many of us, this parable of the Last Judgment strikes us like a blast of cold air when we leave our warm homes in the winter. It frightens us and makes us uncomfortable. We would like to believe that our commitment to our church and our faith, how we teach our children, and the fact that our God is loving and gracious is enough to assure us of eternal life. But once again, much like the story of the rich young ruler, Jesus reaches down into our souls and teaches us about the cost of our discipleship.

This parable, like none other, causes us to turn inward, examine our own motives, reconsider our stereotypes, and move forward into a new ministry. Believing is not enough. Hungry people need more than food stamps; they need an invitation to eat at our table. Thirsty people need more than a cup of water; they need the Living Water. The strangers our parents taught us to fear need to be seen as Christ. People who have no clothing need to be invited into the closets of those of us who "can't find anything to wear." Those who are ill and shut-in need the love and care of a community. Prisoners need us—you and me—to visit them and to offer a human touch in an inhuman situation. But how can we possibly meet these demands? Perhaps, if we look carefully at the parable, we will find that Jesus was addressing someone else.

The parable tells us that the Messiah will separate the sheep from the goats. Sheep were white and goats were black at the time of this parable and they could be separated easily. Even at dusk, when images might appear to be gray and shadowy, a shepherd could identify and separate the sheep from the goats. Appearances were not deceiving.

Many of us stop right here. Most of us have a difficult time leaving the judgment to the Messiah. We prefer to make the judgments ourselves. After all, we know that people who need food stamps are simply too lazy to work. Or are they? Perhaps a single mother has no job training or, having found a job, is unable to afford day care for her children. People in prison deserve to be there. Or do they? Some might, while others simply cannot afford proper legal defense or bail. Street people are simply social misfits. Do you know any?

Very early one morning, when I was in the pastorate, I received a call from the police department. I was asked to give a young couple a place to sleep for the night. Their landlord was crazy and had thrown them out. Other than noticing that the woman was pregnant, I knew nothing about them.

On another occasion, while serving the same church, I was working in the church office and I looked up to discover a woman standing in front of my desk. Her family had put her on a bus from Wyoming to Baltimore with a one-way ticket, no money, and no clothes. They were tired of her. At one time she had rented from a member of our congregation. The former landlady was deceased. Where was she to go? Some street people are mentally ill, released from an institution, with no employment, no food, and no shelter. Families don't want them and most communities shout "NO!" when mental health groups try to open halfway houses in their neighborhoods.

Perhaps God is wise to leave judgment in the hands of the Messiah and not ours. There is an old verse which goes . . .

There is so much good in the worst of us,
And there is so much bad in the best of us,
That it hardly becomes any of us
To talk about the rest of us. (Author unknown)
                    (*Matthew*, The Interpreter's Commentary)

Judgment belongs in God's hands. The Messiah alone separates the sheep from the goats—the blessed from the unblessed.

And, as though that weren't frustrating enough, we become even more upset at the measuring stick used for the judgment: our actions toward those in need. The Messiah declares those on the right as blessed and names them as inheritors of the kingdom, children of God: they fed the hungry, offered drink to the thirsty, invited the stranger, clothed the naked, cared for the sick, and visited the prisoners. They cared not only for those in need but also for the Messiah. For God created all of us and, as we care for God's creation, we care for God. There is something of God in every living thing.

But the blessed did not realize what they had done. They asked, "When?" That question leads us to another realization about the last judgment. Good works, in and of themselves, do not determine one's salvation. One's heart and one's motive stand more clearly in the dividing of the sheep and the goats than do the actions themselves. The blessed cared for those in need, not because they were needy but because they were driven by God's selfless love to respond. "Perhaps, after all, the basic point of Jesus' parable is the *unself-consciousness* of service done in love even more than the division between 'good' and 'bad' or the service rendered in love" (Anna Mow, *Say Yes to Life*, pp. 106-107).

Perhaps we see too many choices. Perhaps we lavish too much time and money on ourselves and creature comforts rather than on the homeless or the prisoners. While pastoring a church, I was asked to serve on a local committee to deal with the homeless issue. Since I had taken in two homeless people for short periods of time, I agreed. When we began meeting, it was clear to me that the majority on the committee were not interested in dealing with the problem of homelessness. They wanted the homeless to leave the area and stop panhandling. They did not want to work on safe shelter for the homeless.

But with the proper motivation, we *can* make a difference! I remember two young children, a boy and a girl from an unchurched family, who came regularly to church. They lived with their mother who received welfare. They always dressed themselves and came alone. The boy was hyperactive but rarely received his prescribed medication. The children struggled with how to act in church. Every month, during fellowship meal, they piled their plates full several times and always took some food home. Did they receive hot meals at home? Were they abused? We didn't know for certain. I visited their mother several times but found her unreceptive. One day, neither child showed up. Months later, the boy appeared in a fast-food restaurant where one of our members worked. He ran up and introduced the member to his father. The boy's father thanked the church for seeing that they were okay once a week and giving them a warm meal once a month. They had not been receiving the best care but it had taken time for the court to act.

The church can make a difference for prisoners. Prisoners are human beings caught up in an inhuman system. The greatest need they have is for human contact. "Those who make direct contact with prisoners and their families touch one of the bitterest aspects of incarceration—isolation" (Criminal Justice Reform Statement, Church of the Brethren Annual Conference, 1975). Some prisoners go years with no visit from family or friends. How long have you gone without visiting friends or family? Prisoners are people created by God, the same as you or I. We are not to judge. Regardless of the crime, regardless of the religious background, how can we not reach out with God's love and compassion?

Discussion and Action

1. Central to the last judgment are our motives for ministry. List several ways you have reached out to those in need. For each on your list, name your motive. Does your motive vary according to circumstances or the person? Are your motive and your response connected?

2. Often, what holds us back from reaching out to people in need are the stereotypes we hold and the judgments we make against them. Read over the list of those in need in Matthew 25:31-46. List your stereotypes and judgments about each group. Discuss which group you struggle with the most? How might you reach out?

3. What are some of the fears you have had about prisoners? What new information have you learned? Are there ways you can reach out to those in prison?

4. What new understanding have you gained about the last judgment? Then, what new commitment are you willing to make?

6

Should Offenders Be Punished?
Exodus 22:1; Leviticus 19:17-18

Preparation

1. Read Exodus 22:1-4 and Leviticus 19:17-18 in a study Bible. What do you believe to be the purpose of these laws? How would you compare them with the laws we have today?
2. Write three descriptions of what you believe a prison environment to be like. Have you had personal experience, read a book, seen a movie, or are you guessing?
3. Reflect on why we have prisons. List some of your reasons and rank them in importance. Be prepared to share this information with the group.

Understanding

Should offenders be punished? One day while I was shopping in a grocery store I thought I witnessed a man, whom I knew to be a street person, slip a package of cheese inside his coat. Should I report it? After all, as a Christian, should I not have compassion on this street person? One package of cheese wouldn't break the grocer. But shouldn't I be honest with the grocer about what I saw? Surprised by the experience and a bit unsure of what I saw (a convenient excuse), I decided against it.

A couple of days later the same man came to the church with a friend asking for food. The receptionist buzzed me. When I recognized him, I told him I was unwilling to assist people who took advantage of others. He looked puzzled and asked for an explanation. I replied that I had seen him take the package of cheese. He and his friend ran out the door and I never saw him again. Should I now report what I *knew* to be true so the offender could be punished?

One morning the kitchen manager of Meals-On-Wheels awakened me in the parsonage with a phone call reporting a break-in at the church. I dressed and rushed over. The church had not only been broken into but also the intruder, still sleeping on the couch in the balcony, was discovered by the custodian. The young man damaged a window, three doors, and dented one of the brass altar vases. When the police awakened him, he remembered nothing about where he was or what he had done. The police filed charges. Should the offender be punished?

Perhaps our answer to that question depends somewhat on our definition of punishment. *Webster's New World Dictionary* defines punishment in two ways. First, punishment is defined as "a penalty imposed on an offender for a crime or wrongdoing." Given this definition, most of us would agree that offenders require punishment.

Secondly, Webster defines punishment as "harsh or injurious treatment." Considering this definition, many of us may not agree that offenders require punishment. Certainly, the laws of the Old Testament teach that there are penalties for offending one's neighbor and even one's enemy (see Exodus 23:4-5). But those laws, such as the ones included in this session, call not for harsh treatment but for restitution, restoration of what was. As we might remember from the first session, central to the theme of justice are right relationships with God and each other and wholeness. Just punishment, then, would not seek harsh treatment but rather restoration of the relationships damaged by the offender. Thus, if a man steals an ox or a sheep from someone, the penalty considered seeks to restore the relationship between the thief and the victim.

How? According to Exodus 22:1, the penalty for stealing an ox and killing it or selling it stood at five oxen. The penalty for stealing a sheep and killing it or selling it stood at four sheep. (Restitution for oxen was higher because they were more likely to be stolen.) It would seem that the penalty *more* than restores what was taken. But it is, after all, a penalty. Remember, also, the inconvenience the victim experienced. Should the offender experience *no* inconvenience? So indeed, the offender is penalized *and* the relationship restored.

Leviticus 19:17-18 adds yet another reminder to this process. "Do not hate your brother [sister] in your heart. Rebuke your neighbor frankly so you will not share in his [or her] guilt. Do not seek revenge or bear a grudge against one of your people, but love your neighbor as yourself (NIV). The Israelites were to be honest about their feelings, settle issues, make restitution, and allow the matter to rest. Doing less resulted in sharing the sin of the offender. Seeking greater penalties resulted in taking revenge. Neither course of action allowed for the restoration of relationships. Such behavior was not in the interest of justice.

As stated in chapter two, prisons are a sign of a rich society. Only rich societies can afford to lock up those whom we consider offensive to society. But what are we accomplishing? In "Alternatives to Failure" (Educational Resources on Criminal Justice, Judicial Process Commission, 1976), four possible objectives have been suggested for maintaining prisons. First, we maintain prisons to punish offenders of more serious crimes. Some studies suggest, however, that half of the men and women in jails and prisons across this nation have committed nonviolent crimes. Many have no prior records and are convicted of minor property-related offenses, such as common theft.

Secondly, we maintain prisons in order to protect citizens and their property. Do they? As we have learned, 95% return to society. And though the poor and minorities constitute the majority of the prison population, white collar crime is eleven times more costly, rarely dealt with, and rarely results in confinement. Some would argue that such crime is less violent. But can we truly say that corporations that dump harmful chemicals illegally, causing premature death and defects in babies, are less violent?

Thirdly, we maintain prisons as deterrents. It is true that for a few of us prison may act as a deterrent—but not for most. Most murder victims are killed because of strong emotional ties with a family member or friend. According to those statistics, we are most vulnerable to murder when in the company of family and friends. Most violent crimes occur in the anger of a moment and, for those crimes, the threat of prison is not a deterrent. We also remember that the recidivism rate, the rate by which people will return to prison, is between 40-60%.

Finally, rehabilitation is the objective often thought of for prisons. Many prison administrators, however, will freely tell you that prisons do not rehabilitate. Indeed, when the majority of money goes for administration, security, and building maintenance, how can rehabilitation even begin to occur? It is not uncommon for a prisoner serving several years to learn more about crime during incarceration. When released, finding no community support, having no job and no one willing to hire an ex-con, the individual will frequently return to criminal behavior.

Hope will never exist for those in prison, conditions will never change, until we who are not in prison demand it. The church's challenge is to be at the center of that kind of change. God challenges us to restore the biblical vision of justice. Prisoners, too, are our neighbors. Jesus calls us to love our neighbors as ourselves. Victims hurt as well, and our love needs to embrace both the victim and the offender as we work at restoring relationships. "Love your neighbor as yourself" stands before us as a demand, not a request.

Discussion and Action

1. After reading the scriptures for this session, do you believe offenders should be punished? How do you define punishment?

2. Leviticus 19:18 reminds us to "love our neighbor as ourselves." Have you ever been the victim of a crime? If so, how did it feel? If not, do you know someone who has? In that situation, is it possible to work at restoring relationships? How?

3. Given the four reasons why we have prisons, which do you believe? Is that objective accomplished by the present system? What might you do to change the system?

4. Many prisoners long for a human contact. Dietrich Bonhoeffer in *Letters and Papers from Prison* compares prison life to advent. "Life in a prison cell reminds me a great deal of advent—one waits and hopes and putters about, but in the end what we do is of little consequence, for the door is shut, and it can only be opened from the outside." That entry is dated November 21, 1943, but many of those same feelings remain today. How can you respond to this need?

7

Reassessing the Death Penalty
Exodus 21:22-25

Preparation

1. Most people, at some point in their lives, have had an urge to retaliate or "get back" at someone. Write down the circumstances of a time when you wanted to retaliate. Who was involved? What was your response—did you retaliate? Was it "an eye for an eye"? Did your retaliation offer you or the other person a sense of *shalom*? Have you since reached a point of wholeness with that person?
2. Reflect on this bumper-sticker question: "Why do we kill people who kill people to show that killing people is wrong?"
3. Do you agree or disagree with the use of the death penalty? List your reasons why or why not.

Understanding

Which of us has not read "eye for eye, tooth for tooth, hand for hand, foot for foot" and not been reminded of a time in our lives when we sought retaliation? Which of us has not had the urge to strike back when we were mistreated or had something that was precious to us damaged or destroyed? After all, the Bible says, "eye for eye, tooth for tooth," doesn't it?

This portion of scripture, known as *lex talionis*, or the law of retaliation, occurs four times in the scriptures. It is first found in Exodus 21:24, repeated in Leviticus 24:19-20 and Deuteronomy 19:21, and referred to by Jesus in Matthew 5:38. The meaning appears very simple and straightforward: Whatever I do to someone, I can expect to have someone do to me, and whatever someone does to me, I may do to them. Thus, proponents of the death penalty reason if someone takes a life, their life should be taken.

Although the meaning appears simple and straightforward, appearances can be deceiving. *Lex talionis* (the law of retaliation) is frequently misunderstood as a legal concept and can only be fully understood in view of Israelite history and law. Clearly, retaliation has a place in Israelite law, but how and when it was allowed are questions needing to be examined.

We know that the death penalty was a part of Israelite law. The Old Testament lists eighteen offenses punishable by death including kidnapping, practicing magic, offering sacrifices to any god other than the Lord, working on the Sabbath, committing adultery, cursing God, committing murder, disobeying a judge or a priest, or being a stubborn and rebellious son. In the midst of such penalties comes the words of Exodus 21:24, "eye for eye, tooth for tooth, hand for hand, foot for foot."

This law of retaliation, widely held in ancient society and found in such ancient laws as the Code of Hammurabi, was first an attempt to provide equality before the law. Although laws existed, many of the wealthy people were treated differently under the law (not unlike our present criminal justice system). An "eye for an eye" cut through economic and social status providing an equality which before did not exist.

Yet another function of this law of retaliation was to limit the retribution that could be exacted for any particular offense. Israelites viewed this matter of retaliation much differently than we do today.

> Today, we define vengeance as revenge, a "paying back" of wrong. In early Hebrew history, this was not so. Rather, vengeance meant the restoration of wholeness and integrity to the community, by God, and at times through people. Vengeance was not vindictive but rather sought to repay or provide restitution for the one violated. Crime was seen as an act against a person, not the state. The Hebrew word for restitution or repayment is *shalam*, the same root as *shalom*, which describes a community characterized by wholeness, justice, right relationships, and peace. Cries to God for vengeance, therefore, are cries for redemption, restoration, health, and healing (Criminal Justice Reform Statement, 1975 Annual Conference, Church of the Brethren).

"An eye for an eye and a tooth for a tooth" does not demand that retaliation take place but places a limit so that no more than an eye can be taken. Furthermore, Deuteronomy 17:6-7 restricts the use of the death penalty requiring two or more witnesses to the offense. In Israelite law, the death penalty was not a punishment but rather a means of restoring relationships—a final attempt to bring about redemption for the victim, the offender, and the community.

Beyond this understanding of Israelite law which may cause us to reassess our own justification of the present day use of the death penalty, John Leith, from Union Theological Seminary, in a paper entitled "Theological Reflections on the Death Penalty," suggests four theological considerations against the death penalty. First, it is difficult to reconcile the death penalty with the preciousness and mystery of human life which comes as a gift from God. How can we deliberately take that which God has given to each created being—the very breath of life? Second, human beings, as creatures, are limited with regard to the human mind and heart. Is any human being wise enough to make the decision to rationally and intentionally take the life of another human being? Certainly, judgments are required to maintain society—judgments tempered with modesty. Third, the use of the death penalty and human sinfulness need to be reconciled. All fall short in the sight of God. Fourth, the death penalty needs to be reconciled with the optimism of grace. How can we arrogantly determine that a human life has no future possibilities?

The law of retaliation at many points in our lives is a law of natural instinct. When I was a probation officer in Indiana, I received a call that a girl had been sexually abused by her stepfather. My first reaction was to have the authorities lock him up. No punishment the system could hand out seemed severe enough. But did such a reaction bring any redemption to the girl or the stepfather or the community?

On another troublesome occasion, I was awakened at 1 a.m., by my neighbors fighting. I called the police and told them of the disturbance. I called them again at 1:30, 2:30, and 3 a.m. By the time of the fifth phone call, I was very angry. I threatened to mow the grass the next morning at 6 a.m., just so those neighbors could be awakened as I had been most of the night. But would such a reaction bring any redemption for myself or anyone else involved?

Redemption, wholeness, justice, healing, relief, salvation: Israelite law worked toward these ends within the community. How can we work for less?

Discussion and Action

1. Read the following scriptures: Exodus 21:12-32; 22:18-21; 35:2; Leviticus 20:1-7, 10, 27; 24:15-21; Deuteronomy 17:6-7, 12; 19:11-13, 20-21; 21:18-21; 22:22-24. List offenses for which the death penalty was prescribed. Are any of these offenses that you have committed? Be honest with yourself.

2. John Leith suggests four theological considerations that weigh against the death penalty. If you are a proponent of the death penalty, how do you reconcile these considerations? If you are an opponent of the death penalty, what are you doing to witness to that fact? Where do members of your congregation stand? Take an informal poll to share next week.

3. What do you know about the death penalty in your own state? Does your state allow for the death penalty? If so, how many people are on death row? How many executions have taken place? Where? When? How? If not, are there officials who have been instrumental in working against such legislation? Many states have a National Coalition Against the Death Penalty chapter. Does yours? Discover some facts. Be prepared to share them next week.

4. What are your assumptions about people in prison? Are those assumptions based on fact or fiction? What do you imagine it would be like to be in prison? To be on death row?

5. What do your beliefs concerning grace, redemption, the giftedness of life, and Jesus Christ dying for the sins of all have to do with the whole matter of reassessing the death penalty?

6. Consider finding a way to reach out to prisoners and/or victims of crime. Perhaps you would consider joining a local chapter of the National Coalition Against the Death Penalty to work against the death penalty or joining the Death Row Support Project to correspond with a prisoner on death row.

8

Response to Personal Injury
Matthew 5:38-42

Preparation

1. Read Matthew 5:38-42. Writers have interpreted these teachings in a variety of ways. Some believe they are to be taken literally. Others believe Jesus' teachings dare not be taken literally or all of us would simply be naked and broke. Rather, Jesus teaches that we should be generous and our attitudes kind. How do you interpret these teachings of Jesus?
2. Take some time as a group to share the facts you discovered about the death penalty.

Understanding

As I was growing up in the church, I heard the "social gospel" preached again and again. There I learned that God *is* Love and Jesus, the personification of God's love, lives as our example of true love. Indeed, some, believing so strongly that God loved all people, struggled with the concept of hell and the judgment of God. Yet, when one of my closest friends dated a black youth, I heard a family in that same church tell their preschool child not to play with "that kind." When another of my friends in the church became pregnant out of wedlock, she felt ostracized from the community of faith with little, if any, love and compassion extended. Unfortunately, those are *not* isolated incidents that have happened in one church. Those incidents multiply to include most of our churches, and if we are honest most of us feel somewhat the same way.

Often we preach and teach God's radical, all-encompassing love, yet we practice a much more moderate, safe kind of love that doesn't "rock the boat." In the introduction to the book *The Upside-Down Kingdom* by Donald Kraybill, John Alexander reminds us:

> Jesus is very popular. Most everyone thinks He's one of the great moral teachers of all times. It's okay to criticize Marx or Adam Smith, Roosevelt or Barry Goldwater. But hardly anyone ever criticizes Jesus. Or obeys Him. In fact, we go to great lengths claiming He didn't teach what He clearly did. We have to, of course. To admit He taught what He did would require us either to change (repent) or to criticize Him. And neither of those is acceptable (Herald Press, p. 13).

Jesus is an extremist. Most of us are moderates. Jesus called for a radical tearing down and rebuilding of one's life (being born again). We feel our lives are basically okay. We simply need a little polishing. Or as Alexander puts it, "A tune-up will do the job: be kinder to those we're closest to, give another $50 a month to relief, work for blacks to move into our neighborhood." Or does Jesus call us to more than that?

In the Sermon on the Mount, Jesus issues a clear call to more than a moderate "tuning up" of our lives. Here, Jesus reinterprets the law. He teaches all who would follow a Christian life of discipleship and love that fulfilling the law is not sufficient. Rather, we are called to go beyond the requirements of the law. Jesus states, "For I tell you, unless your righteousness exceeds that of the scribes and Pharisees, you will never enter the kingdom of heaven" (Matt. 5:20).

As we learned in the last chapter, the law limited retaliation. This law of retaliation ranges from interpersonal situations to international crises. When I was growing up, I sensed that if my younger sister decided to pinch me, justice demanded that I pinch her. If Libya bombs a nightclub in Germany where Americans are killed, certainly America has the right to bomb Libya. This course of retaliation not only permits "an eye for an eye" but may also allow for an excess of the original insult so that a "lesson can be learned." So, not only may I pinch my sister, I can make it an extra hard pinch so she won't forget her crime. America may bomb not only one location but several, so Libya will not forget her crime.

But Jesus teaches that this fulfillment of the law, though it provides for God's requirements, falls short of God's true intentions.

Jesus never declares that the law is wrong—simply inadequate. The only adequate response for any act against us, according to Jesus, is the strength from God to love in spite of what's happened.

For most of us, however, we dare not take the teachings of Jesus too literally. After all, they are impractical, idealistic, and too costly. We can explain them away in a variety of ways. For if we followed them, we would find ourselves insulted, beaten, naked, cold, broke, homeless—all situations Jesus himself experienced. If Jesus had wanted us to interpret these teachings in a moderate way, would he not have lived them in a moderate way? Jesus so challenged the thinking of the moderates in his day that eventually the authorities killed him.

Indeed Jewish thinking had already changed. The death penalty, though allowed in biblical laws, could rarely be carried out. Many restrictions, including the number of eye witnesses required, prohibited the use of the death penalty except in rare cases. But even with this moderation in thinking and this focus on the fairness of the law, Jesus taught that the law of love was even more radical. The law of love extended beyond fairness, beyond moderation.

Moderation was not in Jesus' mind when he said, "Do not resist one who is evil. But if any one strikes you on the right cheek, turn to him the other also; and if any one would sue you and take your coat, let him have your cloak as well; and if any one forces you to go one mile, go with him two miles. Give to him who begs from you, and do not refuse him who would borrow from you" (Matt. 5:39-40). Though the law requires less, Jesus knows the law of love requires as much. Such love demands radical changes in our attitudes and lives.

Jesus knows the difficult task to which he calls us. In Jewish culture, a blow on the right cheek symbolized the greatest possible contempt and abuse one could experience. It was an act punishable by a fine equivalent to more than a year's wages (*The Upside-Down Kingdom*, p. 215). Jesus teaches love, not retaliation, as the response to the most abusive insult. Jesus shows us that love stands higher than any law or custom.

So what would Jesus have us to do? Shall we give money to every beggar who approaches? If we did, we would be broke! John Alexander reminds us: " . . . maybe our being broke is exactly what Jesus had in mind. The reason we find being broke so unthinkable is because our culture finds it unthinkable, not because it's unchristian" (*The Upside-Down Kingdom*, p. 17). Perhaps we should take time to find them a meal. Then we would never accomplish all our busywork! Maybe that is what Jesus had in mind. Should we freely loan out our possessions to anyone who asks? Then we would never have things available for ourselves! We would always be inconvenienced!

This means that when it comes to interpersonal as well as international crises we might rethink our responses. We can work for a systemic change in a criminal justice system that puts law above love, punishment above people. We can commit ourselves to turning the other cheek, walking the second mile, and offering ourselves as well as our possessions to our friends and our families.

Discussion and Action

1. What do you believe is the basis and motive for the teachings of Jesus? How is it possible to live according to these teachings of Jesus and be a part of our culture?
2. Think of an interpersonal relationship with which you are struggling. If you were to put these verses from Matthew into action, what might your response be?
3. How might a current international situation be responded to using these verses from Matthew and your own faith beliefs?
4. Can you integrate your beliefs about the death penalty and these teachings of Jesus? How can the law of love influence the law of the land? How can punishment and compassion be dealt at the same time?
5. As a group list all the responses to Matthew 5:38-42, and select a writer from the group to summarize the responses in a letter to your congresspersons. During the next session sign it as a group and mail it.

9

Embracing the Victims
Luke 10:25-37

Preparation

1. Read Luke 10:25-37. Compare Matthew 22:34-40 and Mark 12:28-34. How do the questions compare? Are there differences? Why?
2. The lawyer in Luke says, "Teacher, what shall I do to inherit eternal life?" What is the lawyer really asking? Have you ever asked the same question? How has Jesus answered you?
3. Look for the characters in this parable as you interact with others this week. Who are the robbers? Who are the wounded? Do you know priests and Levites? Who are the Samaritans today?

Understanding

If we were to rank the five most read stories in the Bible, we would certainly rank the Good Samaritan among the top five. We sometimes tire of seeking new meanings for this frequently read passage. And at times we even tire of hearing the old meanings. After all, how many times can a person read a story and discover something new? Every time! And sometimes, we simply need a reminder of what has always been. This particular scripture passage appears to me like a kaleidoscope with a unique beauty for each turn made in the story. The beauty can never be seen apart from viewing the twists and turns of each perspective.

One such perspective comes from the lawyer. Perhaps the lawyer heard about the return of the seventy who had been preaching and casting out demons. This man had spent his life following the law, loving God, and caring for his family and friends. Was something more required? Was his righteous living not enough? Intent on proving his right to eternal life, he said to Jesus, "Teacher, what shall I do to inherit eternal life?" The lawyer hoped that by defining the limits of his duty and showing how he had fulfilled those duties, he had earned the right to eternal life. But eternal life is no one's *right* and salvation can never be earned—it is a matter of faith! Eternal life is grace and salvation cannot be calculated.

The priest and the Levite give us another perspective. The priest represented the highest religious leadership among the Jews. The Levite was the designated lay-associate of the priest. Priests and Levites were not expected to live in Jerusalem when off duty. Since they were traveling between Jerusalem and Jericho, we might assume they were off duty. We might also expect them, being religious people, to show concern and care for persons in need. Yet they walked by on the other side.

Concern for someone is sometimes not enough. Fears sometimes outweigh concern. Leviticus 21:1-3 tells us that the priest had a particular dilemma. If the man would die in the priest's hands, the priest would be disbarred from the priesthood for life. (That's enough to make most of us stop and think about whether or not we should help! Many of us refuse to help for fear of being sued.)

Why didn't they help? For the same reasons many of us would not help—fear, the calculation of risk was too high, prejudice, ignorance—to name a few. If you wish to list all the reasons, simply list the reasons you offer when you choose not to help. But remember, the reason why they chose not to stop matters little. The fact is that they *chose* not to stop and help one who was hurting. The neighbor is defined not by intentions, not by faith, but rather by the uncalculated actions of one who loves.

Now let us turn to the Samaritan, a foreigner not expected to show sympathy *or* compassion to a Jew. John 4:9 notes the relationship between the Samaritans and Jews. "For Jews have no dealings with Samaritans." In one tradition (Matt. 10:5), Jesus charges the disciples not to enter a Samaritan village. Samaria was inhabited by mixed remnants of the northern tribes. Jews regarded them as mongrels.

So here was a foreigner in hostile territory, walking by a complete stranger—a victim who was stripped, beaten, and almost dead. Most of us would turn and look the other way. But the Samaritan, out of love, showed compassion. It was love that was uncalculated and unrestrained. The oil and wine used as healing agents were not dabbed on but poured on the wounds of the stranger. Transportation wasn't flagged down and begged from someone else; the Samaritan used his own beast, paid his own money for the inn, and provided personal care. Never does the story indicate that the response was out of a sense of duty. Indeed, the Samaritan had no awareness of duty but rather offered the gift of mercy.

Mercy, according to the lawyer, defined the Samaritan as neighbor. Jesus commands the lawyer, "Go and do likewise" (Luke 10:37). In order to *do* likewise, we must learn to extend mercy—first to ourselves, then to others. We can never extend it to others beyond our learning to extend it to ourselves. We may never love our neighbor more than we love ourselves. Jesus demands we love them as much.

But the question remains, "Who is our neighbor?" Our neighbor is anyone in need. Our neighbor is a victim. Victims need many things. Often, victims need someone to listen to their fears, their anger, their guilt. Listening occurs not only at the moment of trauma, but also for days, weeks, and sometimes even years. In the moment of crisis, many victims need someone to lead them through the next steps. Often victims need someone to assist them in realizing their own worth and power at a time when they feel worthless and powerless. Victims need someone who will point out options but not someone who decides on solutions.

The parable of the Good Samaritan calls us to reach out to our neighbors who are victims. Webster defines a victim as "someone or something killed, destroyed, injured, or otherwise harmed by or suffering from some act, condition, agency, or circumstance." Given this definition, most of us are victims at one time or another in our lives whether a crime is involved or not.

Many of us hesitate to reach out to the victims in our world. We would almost rather *be* the victim than be asked to reach out *to* the victim. Perhaps, victims remind us that we, too, are victims. Our neighbor is anyone who requires our *active* love—not simply our feelings of compassion. More than offering a bandaid or instructions, our neighbor is one who needs *us* to bind the wounds so that healing can occur. We need to confess our wounds to one another. We need to listen to one another and live with our wounds. Jesus calls us to offer much more than a bandaid; he calls us to offer ourselves.

Perhaps to gain the full impact of this story we can reflect on an actual experience that happened in the Middle East. A traveler in the

Middle East witnessed an automobile accident in which a pedestrian was hurt. Getting out of his car, he tried to help. He noticed the crowd getting somewhat unruly, and when the police came they told him to leave immediately. The man indicated he did not mind helping but the police insisted that he leave. So he did. Feeling very upset, he stopped at the police station in the next town to report what had happened. The police laughed at him. In the Middle East culture, it was not appropriate to help a complete stranger. To do so could lead to one's death.

What happened to the Samaritan when he left the inn? We never know. Might people have killed this foreigner who helped a complete stranger? We never know. Regardless of the cost, Jesus calls us to reach out in love to victims—any person in need—not with a bandaid but with our whole being.

Discussion and Action

1. We refer to this story as the "good" Samaritan. Do we call the Samaritan "good" because he stops or does he stop because he is good?

2. The scripture tells us that the Samaritan had compassion. How do you define compassion? What is the source of compassion?

3. Who are the victims in our society today? Are there victims in your community? Who are the wounded in your faith community? How have you been wounded?

4. When considering this story, many of us are sidetracked by the question of whether we would pick up a hitchhiker. Without becoming sidetracked on this question, talk about how you can minister both individually and corporately to the wounded you have named above.

5. Today's criminal justice system is not focused on the victim but on punishment. Do victims receive any benefits from our present system? How could victims benefit from forms of punishment other than incarceration?

10

Living an Alternative
Isaiah 61:1-3; Luke 4:14-30

Preparation

1. Read Isaiah 61:1-3 and Luke 4:14-30. In what ways are these two passages identical? What are the differences?
2. You will note that Jesus quoted only a portion of the Isaiah scripture. Why do you think he stopped where he did? What did he add? Why? What would the response of your family and friends be to this sermon preached by Jesus?
3. Do you believe Jesus intended that his words be taken literally or symbolically? If symbolic, what do they mean?

Understanding

We end our study where we began—with the prophet Isaiah. If taken literally, most of us find that these words of scripture in Isaiah and Luke alarm and threaten us. When taken literally, they call for social revolution—not from the bottom up but from the top, down. Certainly Jesus could not have intended that! After all, in the economic and social structures of the world, we find *ourselves* on the top.

We tend to spiritualize the meaning of this passage. Typically we understand Jesus to say that we are to preach good news to the poor in spirit, release the captives of sin, recover sight for the spiritually blind, and set free those oppressed by evil. But in accepting this we fail to capture the vision of Jesus.

Donald Kraybill, in *The Upside-Down Kingdom*, responds, "While this is true, the Old Testament background to the text enriches and expands its meaning considerably." André Trocmé shows that the "acceptable year of the Lord" refers to the Old Testament Jubilee. Thus Jesus was actually announcing that the kingdom of God was a restoration of the Hebrew Jubilee. The year of the Jubilee established practices that promoted wholeness and well-being for all members of society. It demanded justice borne out of a compassionate love for all people.

The Hebrews celebrated, as many of us do, the familiar pattern of a six-day work week with the seventh day being a day of rest. This pattern developed from the creation story where God rested on the seventh day. The Hebrew calendar did not stop here, however. They also counted years. After working six years, they celebrated the seventh year as a year of rest—a sabbatical year. After seven sabbatical years, they celebrated a Jubilee year.

Practices of sabbatical and Jubilee years turned Hebrew society upside-down. Land lay fallow as crops were not planted or harvested. The poor took any volunteer plants (Exod. 23:10, 11; Lev. 25:2-7). Slaves gained their freedom. Most became slaves because of debts they owed and, after working six years, freedom was theirs (Exod. 21:1-6; Deut. 15:12-18). Debts, which were mostly charitable loans rather than commercial loans, were cancelled (Deut. 15:1-6). During the Jubilee year (the fiftieth year), one other practice was observed. Land reverted back to original occupants (Lev. 25:10). Such practices surely called for social revolution—but from the top down. Why would God propose this revolution from the top down?

For our understanding, Donald Kraybill suggests six underlying principles for the sabbatical and Jubilee practices (*The Upside-Down Kingdom*, pp. 101-105). First, God owns all human and natural resources, not people! "The land and the people are the Lord's! They are not to be used in any careless fashion . . . . They dare not be used to build up huge economic pyramids and social dynasties."

Secondly, God's action to liberate is at the heart of Jubilee practices. God decided to liberate the Hebrews from Egypt. It was God's act, and the repetition of that history for the Hebrew people stands at the heart of their faith. At one time, they were slaves, foreigners, crying out for freedom. God heard their cries, intervened, and liberated them.

Thirdly, there is the Jubilee response. As the history is remembered and repeated, the only response is to joyously pass on the gift of liberation. But simply freeing the slave was not enough. God's redemption was liberal, so must theirs be. "And when you let him go free from you, you shall not let him go empty-handed; you shall furnish him liberally out of your flock, out of your threshing floor, and out of your wine press; as the Lord your God has blessed you, you shall give to him" (Deut. 15:13-14).

The fourth element is Jubilee compassion. A recitation of history falls short. One eye and the heart look to the future as well as to present abuses of those crushed by the economic and social structures. Witnessing the oppression of the ones trampled reminds the celebrant of their own slavery.

As we have already mentioned, the fifth element is an upside-down revolution. Kraybill writes, "Those in power, the rich and influential, are moved by God's grace. They see with compassionate eyes and join the Jubilee by periodically redistributing the control of natural and human resources. The socio-economic pyramids are flattened out. Those at the top begin freely giving as God has given them" (p. 104).

Finally, the sixth principle is institutionalized grace. As human sin and greed grow, the pyramid effect on society grows with it. Without the periodic leveling, the poor and oppressed become poorer and more oppressed. The sabbatical and Jubilee years become institutionalized grace.

For those gathered to hear Jesus preach, the inaugural sermon contained old words with a new meaning. Earlier words foretold of the Messiah. On that day, the Messiah was announced. "Today this scripture has been fulfilled in your hearing" (Luke 4:21). Later in Luke, when John sends his disciples to inquire whether Jesus is the Messiah, the same listing is used. Jesus refuses to offer a definite yes or no. Rather he responds with, "Go and tell John what you have seen and heard: the blind receive their sight, the lame walk, lepers are cleansed, and the deaf hear, the dead are raised up, the poor have good news preached to them" (Luke 7:22). The principles of Jubilee are the work of the Messiah; both restore wholeness and well-being for all members of society.

But it is not enough to understand what Jesus spoke to the people in his own synagogue. What are *we* to do with those words? Are we to begin the practice of sabbatical and Jubilee years? No. But we might ask ourselves what is *our* response to God's act? Kraybill writes, "Now we remember that we are forgiven debtors. We are released slaves. One time we were oppressed. One time we were captives" (p. 107). The reciprocal history that led Hebrews to celebrate the Jubilee is ours to celebrate as well. Jesus calls us, as well, to pass on the acceptable year of the Lord—the year of Jubilee.

God's liberating grace in our lives demands social consequences! Isaiah's vision of a peaceable world—a world in which everyone and everything fits rightly and is treated justly—demands our action. We fall far short if all we do is sit and reflect on the wonder of God's grace. Certainly prayer and forgiveness of interpersonal insults have their place but they are not enough! We must not only pray for the homeless, those on welfare, and the hungry, but also build homes, lower rents, and feed the hungry. God's people, regardless of race or sexual orientation, are to be accepted and included in our faith community and the world. How can we take seriously the words of Jesus and fail to see our faith and actions, love and justice, mercy and power, all tied up together?

Being obedient to the words of Jesus does not mean we duplicate the Jubilee. But those same principles can instruct our lives and our faith. If we follow those principles, we will find ways to share with those in poverty, release those in prison, enable the blind to see, and free the oppressed.

Discussion and Action

1. The history associated with the Jubilee year is a rhythm passed down through time. It begins with God's perfect freedom, moves to our oppression, follows with God's intervention, and we respond. How have you experienced that pattern in your life?

2. Can the principles from the Jubilee year inform your response to the grace you have received? How?

3. Do you see God's grace (love) in your life and social action (justice) as intertwined? How?

4. What ways can you find to be part of the upside-down revolution?